Speaking For Myself

Margaret Eddershaw

Speaking for Myself
published in the United Kingdom in 2024
by Mica Press & Campanula Books

c/o Leslie Bell
47 Belle Vue Road, Wivenhoe, Colchester, Essex CO7 9LD
micapress.uk | contact@micapress.uk

ISBN 978-1-869848-36-1

PREFACE

The Royal Albert Hospital, under its full title "Asylum for Idiots and Imbeciles and the Weak-Minded of Northern England", opened in 1870 in Lancaster. It was renamed the Royal Albert Psychiatric Hospital in 1930 and was closed down in 1996.

The poems in this pamphlet draw primarily on the words of patients and staff at the Royal Albert and of adults with learning difficulties, living in the community and attending Thorpe View Centre in Morecambe. Most of them participated in weekly drama workshops at Lancaster University led by the poet. Their names have been changed.

CONTENTS

Black lines are from Reports of the Royal Albert Hospital Board of Governors, 1870 –1960 (published 1992). Those in italics are words of Royal Albert patients quoted in *Unlocking the Past Archives* (1984).

TOWER OF BABEL

God help
the imbecile!
please listen to this
my never-heard story
all the feeble-minded are
parasitic and very dangerous
I should have total control over
everything that happens in all my life
to avoid degeneracy within our nation
we must keep all our imbeciles separated
I know I have a very slow tongue in my head
but all people must allow me to speak for myself
all the forms of idiot pass their lives in the state
of a prolonged and even an irredeemable infancy
lives of people like us should be made clearly visible
we ought to be a full part of everyone else's daily world
we know that the mentally defective person cannot ever
be allowed to manage alone the living of his or her own life
I know that there are times when I get a bit confused in my head
but I must tell you that I don't think it should be seen as unusual
high-grade imbeciles and idiots in this our modern society are
always potential criminals and so they must be locked up forever
I think that ordinary people assume persons like us lack real abilities
they think we have only challenges, difficulties and serious disabilities
all idiots, imbeciles, the weak-minded and mental defectives must be
eliminated at their birth for the sake of the safety of our whole society
anyone living in the real world would surely go crazy, if they were forced
against their will, like we are, to spend their whole lives in this foul prison!

Julie, a nurse, speaks

NAKED TRUTH

Standing before Michelangelo's fresco
of the *Last Judgment* —
with its jumble of contorted figures
outstretched palms, pleading faces
covered by despairing fingers —
I knew I'd seen similar scenes before.

At the Royal Albert Mental Hospital
I bathed eighty women every Monday
with the aid of one other nurse.
our patients queued up naked
some sitting in wheelchairs
a few with walking-frames,
their sagging, mis-shapen bodies
pale and flabby as raw pastry
the air filled with moans, shrieks
only an occasional laugh.

We lifted them into a huge Victorian bath
sponged four women at a time
in rapidly cooling water.
Some felt threatened
others found meagre enjoyment
in that rare bodily contact
even when rubbed briskly
with the mean, coarse towels.
We joshed and teased
these vulnerable souls
to stave off our own tears.

ROSE'S VIEW

I'm like a Persian cat, says my sister
my flat face
my curled shells for ears
my slanty eyes.

Dad likes my rosebud mouth
but not my large tongue
dangling like a dog panting –
I can do amazing things with it
but they say that's rude.

Mongols, says my Mum,
*that's what they once called
people like you, Rose.*
Fierce, proud people they are
they sleep in yurts
are brilliant horsemen.

I go to riding lessons –
soon I'll be fierce and proud, too
as well as lovely.

Helen's Story

CLOTHED IN SCORN

I wear a shapeless garment
of rough, itchy stuff
great-coat heavy
stiff under the armpits
tight round the limbs
short at the wrists
buttons near their limits.

As I come near, folk look away
pretend not to notice me
or they stare with cold eyes
others cross the road
some back off fast
a few spit on me.

Julie, a nurse, speaks

THE SHEARING

My first week as care-assistant
only fifteen myself,
Isabel was thirteen
fantastic face
golden hair flowing down her back
but her fine limbs
were smeared with excrement.
Her mother fled sobbing –
she couldn't manage her any more.

Staff Nurse grabbed Isabel by the hair
three of them dragged her to the 'security' chair
clamped her arms and legs.

She roared like a wild beast
spat at the nurse
who hacked off her crowning glory
with large, blunt scissors –
lightning-struck corn scattered over the floor.

Someone jeered as if she were a criminal
being prepared for the gallows
shorn then sedated
stripped of all clothes
Isabel was hauled off
to the punishment room.

I'll never forget
the dark pools of her eyes:
a terrified antelope
squealing in the jaws of lions.

CHARLOTTE'S DREAM

Six months now and no visitor for weeks
seen the doctor only once –
my parents brought me here
for one month's treatment, they said.
Father regards my epileptic fits
as weakness on my part,
to Mother I am an embarrassment.

This hospital was a great shock to me.
I have been mightily downcast.
I am in a private ward
with other women whose families pay,
we are always locked in.
I can't read my books
my trunk locked in a storeroom.

Recently, in a dream I was walking
down a corridor in my hand a large key.
I unlocked a door
stepped into an overgrown garden,
like *The Secret Garden*.
Padlocked chests were piled
against a high stone wall
like coffins abandoned in a grave-yard.

There was my trunk.
I found my ribbons, shells, books
folded clothes wrapped in tissue.
I lifted out the blue silk ball-gown
Mother gave me for my 16th birthday
that last week at home.

The dress whispered over my body
soft as spring water.
Suddenly I was back home
in our large reception room
with family and friends all waiting to dance -
but before the music began
I woke up.

MABEL'S REBELLION

Here doors are locked
windows barred
and rules are very strict:
Thou shalt not:
Wear thine own clothes
Leave any room without permission
Talk to or sit with the opposite sex
Converse at meal-times
Neglect domestic chores –
Or thou shall be locked naked
In the padded room.

We crawl back into ourselves,
any resistance by us
requests for understanding
or expression of our opinion
they call "challenging behaviour".

So I sit on the toilet and sing
one of the songs I made up:
They say the Royal Albert's a wonderful place
But the goings on here are a shocking disgrace
And why do they tell me to pull up my socks?
For when I leave here, it will be in a box!

I remember a huge cupboard full of dreadful old knickers that we had to give out. Julie, a nurse.

THE GIVING OUT OF KNICKS
After *The Naming of Parts* by Henry Reed

Today we have giving out knicks. Yesterday
We had weekly bathing. And tomorrow morning
We shall show how to use a toothbrush. But today
Today we have giving out knicks. You women are
Ready to try on calico, nylon and woollen undies
For today we have giving out knicks.

This is the long-legged knicker. And this
Is the higher-cut knicker, whose fit you will see
When you are given a pair. Here are crotchless knicks
Which in your case, you will not wear. The nurses
Are showing you samples with appropriate gestures
Which most of you are unable to understand.

This has the button-up waist that is always released
With an easy twist of the thumb. Please don't let me
See anyone using her finger. You can do it quite easily
If you have any strength in your thumb. These bloomers
Are lace-trimmed and fragile, you must never pull them
Too hard because they will tear.

And these as you can see are the briefs. Their purpose
Is to allow the air to circulate. We can slip such knicks
Easily over the hips leaving the waist quite free, thus
Cooling the body. But if you prefer French knickers
They sit easy on the hip, too, but are longer in the leg
Yet also leave the waist quite free.

We give you plenty of choice of fabric, and fastenings, too:
There are ties or buttons or elastic. We have cami-knickers
And panties and there's even this modern-looking bikini style
Which in your case you may not want; there's double gusset
Or single in the flowered, gingham, wool or just plain cotton
For today we have the giving out of knicks.

A poem based on a transcription from Mary's sign language

MARY'S REBIRTH

Like me
cats make sounds
instead of proper words
and can't read or write.

But they keep their coats clean
with those thistle tongues
trim nails with pointed teeth
sleep as long as they like.

They get fussed with kindness
have many babies – no-one says
to them: *You can't manage!*
Cats decide for themselves.

So when I die
escape this place
I shall be reborn
as a tabby cat.

Norman was taken to the Royal Albert when he was four years old because his mother was sick and there was no-one to care for him. He lived in the hospital for thirty years, before being released.

PIGS IS SMART

A few years back, Peter, a young lad
were put to work with me
caring for t'chickens and pigs.
Poor sod shuffled along like an old bear
head bouncing about as if held on by elastic.

Even chickens thought him strange
but pigs is smart, they work things out.
Now when Peter brings their slop
he speaks in a soft voice
and they understand his problems.

T'lad walks better these days,
head much less wobbly.
After feeding time he chats to Charlie,
our old boar as if they were mates int'pub.

One afternoon last winter I found Peter
curled up asleep inside the pig-pen
head on the belly of a pregnant sow
like she were a huge pink pillow
and I'd swear there was a smile
on both their faces.

FRACTURED WORDS

Pearl, named for a gritty start:
was abandoned in the street, aged two,
and diagnosed as mentally subnormal.
Foster-care enclosed her innocence.

Come twenty, with a lustrous face
Pearl joins our drama classes.
Shy till seeded with confidence
she opens like a pink rose.

She loves sport so she and I
play squash at the university
have coffee afterwards.
One day she confides:
You are my only friend.
When I protest she adds:
The only person in my life
not mental or paid to care.

Drama sessions resume without Pearl.
I ask the staff about her and we stare
into the muddy waters of abuse.
In the park I hold her trembling fingers
piece together her fractured words:
rough hands - torn blouse – hot breath
pushing – struggle – hurt!
I promise my support in court.
Later we rehearse her lines.

But after weeks of spiteful whispering
at the Day Centre
Pearl crept back into her shell.
The male carer moved on.

Elizabeth talks about her life in the Royal Albert Hospital.

MY BOY

I shamed my family, you see
disgraced myself, they said
by not knowing at thirteen
where a roll in the hay could get me.
So after my baby was born
my parents put me in here
left-luggage they never reclaimed.

I'm ninety now
the only one in here still breast-feeding –
he's so bonny is my Jimmy.
One of the nurses makes his clothes.
Good as gold at night he is, never cries,
his tummy grumbles when he's hungry
but that's only normal, isn't it?

Some women in my dormitory
are jealous of me
make bitchy remarks;
only yesterday skinny Susan said:
*I don't know why you walk around
with that grubby old teddy-bear!*

I know what she's up to.

Brian's story of the Royal Albert Scout Troop

BE PREPARED

Of a Thursday, six of us in our uniforms
met our Leader in the Recreation Room;
first we learnt the Scout Promise:
to do our best for God, Queen and others,
we recited the Scout Law that says:
Scouts must do a good deed every day.

Then Mr Peter taught us knots
and all about plants and trees
we even made ourselves beans on toast.

That summer we camped in Silverdale –
we slept in a tent, heard owls hoot
listened to leaves rustling overhead
we fetched water from a stream
built a camp-fire
boiled a billy-can to make tea.

When we came back – bad news.
Chief Scout in London had written a letter
saying boys *like us* could not understand
the Scout Promise and the Scout Law
so our troop had to stop.
We were right upset,
but Mr. Peter couldn't do nowt about it.

Before they snatched back our uniforms
I unpinned the metal badge
with the three curled feathers
hid it in my drawer.
Some nights I take it out
run my thumb along the motto

Be Prepared.
not sure what that means
but I still do a good deed every day.

JANET CAN'T SPEAK

Drama will be good for her, they say
challenging me to break and enter.
She's thirty, they say.
Autistic.

Why not leave Janet in her world
to tear a strip of paper into a spiral
twist it expertly
before intense eyes?

She can't make decisions, they say.
Each week she decides
to shrink from my touch
to sit still while others move
scowl instead of smile.

Will you join our circle, Janet?
After three decades of life
without words
she decides to speak:
No, she says.

JANET'S FINGER & THUMB

                    finger and thumb
                    tear a strip
                    down the edge
                    paper curls

a spiral:

                        twist it round
                    finger and thumb
              shut out
           voices
              faces come close
                  breaking in
                      shatter glass
                  twist it round
              finger and thumb
           breathe in
              the pattern
                  repeat
                    can't hear words
                won't hear
              twist it round
          finger and thumb
              no, don't
                  don't touch
let me
                  twist it round
          finger and thumb

JACK'S COWS

Voices in my head told me do bad things
so they brought me to this dark place
gave me pills to stop those voices
paid me sixpence a week to milk the cows.

Twice a day the herd weaves t't shed
at its own pace nodding, ears flicking
tails swishing side to side
hooves clatter on the stone floor
as the herd skitters into stalls.

They gaze at me with huge wet eyes
push forward their shiny noses
I lean against the warm flank
wipe muck off the udder
pull with a firm rhythm on two teats at once.
Like playing bagpipes Dad used to say.

The cow chews and chews and chews
sways from foot to foot
splatters the floor with steaming heaps
and then, relieved of milk
she tiptoes into the yard.
I pour creamy froth into the churn
move on to the next.

WALTER

When the Royal Albert closed down
Walter was placed in a Morecambe B & B.
He shambled along unfamiliar streets
watched children play in the fairground
sat on the windswept prom waiting for the long tide
to return.
After forty years of institutional living
he was overcome with uncertainty
a hermit crab without a shell.

At the weekly drama session,
he sat with oversize hands clasped tight in his lap
a schoolboy outfaced by a page
he could not read.

Then one day the group enacted
a make-believe bus-trip:
suddenly Walter stood up
declared to the room he loved buses
he tried to hug them when stationary.

For weeks thereafter bus-driver Walter
drove his group on imaginary outings
to Blackpool
to Paris
and to the moon.

MAVIS SPEAKS

I'm blind in my left eye
my right arm is deformed
and my walk has a stutter.

Loony! mutter two old women
as they waddle past.
I don't call them Fatties.

Teenagers teeter across the road
shrieking like gaudy parrots:
Imbecile! Defective! Freak! Cretin!
Their pockets full of stuff
nicked from Boots, I expect.

Lads in the park surround me
like wild dogs slathering:
Subnormal! Insane! Bananas! Retard!
I'm not dumb.
I don't smoke or do drugs.

Everyone has a special gift, don't they?
Remember the Rain Man, I say!

A ROYAL ALBERT MATRON ARRANGES A WEDDING

Alice's Wedding

Brain-damaged when twenty-five
Alice in Wonderland, we call her:
tiny and sweet-faced as a child
her long grey hair held by a band
she spends her days whispering
with invisible friends
including a long-dead ginger cat.

I wonder when my marriage will take place?
After all, I've given birth to a child
so surely there must soon be a wedding!
is her mantra.

We humor Alice: find a loose, white dress
pin a sheet to its shoulders as a train;
Head gardener brings a bunch of flowers
dons his Sunday jacket to play groom.
I provides a brass curtain-ring
coloured confetti is from the art class.

A male nurse escorts the ancient bride
as she zimmer-frames between chairs.
Spontaneous humming of the Bridal March
prompts giggles
but due solemnity is soon achieved
even a few tears.

Lemonade toasts are offered
a Sainsbury's iced sponge
eagerly shared out with cups of tea
till like the dormouse
the bride falls softly asleep
on her slice of cake.

Roger, a 35 year old with Downs Syndrome performed *Hello Dolly!* in a presentation by the Thorpe View drama group. It was part of an international conference on the drama methods of Dorothy Heathcote, held at Lancaster University.

ROGER PERFORMS *HELLO, DOLLY!*

Last look in the mirror:
wig straight, eye-lashes bold, lipstick glossy,
full-length gloves smooth
sequin dress gorgeous
ostrich-feather fan sexy.
Hand-mike ready
all set.

Wait in wings
breathe breathe
listen for cue
step into the follow-spot:

I said, Hello, Dolly!
move slowly downstage
survey the audience –
You're looking swell, Dolly
across the front, up centre aisle
slowly slowly.

You're still going strong –
blow that man a kiss
Find her an empty lap, fellas!
Sit on his lap
You're still glowing
cross to stage left,
give them the fan and mike
slowly pull off a glove.
It's so nice to have you back where you belong
wave glove and take the fan and mike.

Back down centre aisle
I feel the room swaying
careful, don't trip over the dress
hold centre stage
Dolly'll never go away again!
Raise fan high in the air
curtsy curtsy curtsy!!

Milton Keynes UK
Ingram Content Group UK Ltd.
LKHW021538080424
440761UK00002B/2